VAN BUREN

# ENCYCLOPEDIA
# of PRESIDENTS

# *Martin Van Buren*

*Eighth President of the United States*

By Jim Hargrove

*Consultant: Charles Abele, Ph.D.*
*Social Studies Instructor*
*Chicago Public School System*

CHILDRENS PRESS ®

CHICAGO

A daguerreotype
of Martin Van Buren
by early photographer
Mathew Brady

**Library of Congress Cataloging-in-Publication Data**

Hargrove, Jim.
   Martin Van Buren/by Jim Hargrove.
      p.    cm. — (Encyclopedia of presidents)
   Includes index.
   Summary: Examines the life of the lawyer politician who
became the eighth president of the United States and led the
country through its first serious depression.
   ISBN 0-516-01391-2
   1.   Van Buren, Martin, 1782-1862 — Juvenile
literature.   2.   Presidents — United States — Biography —
Juvenile literature.   [1.   Van Buren, Martin, 1782-
1862.   2.   Presidents.]   I.   Title.   II.   Series.
E387.H37    1987
973.5'7'0924 — dc19                            87-16023
[B]                                                CIP
[92]                                                AC

**Picture Acknowledgments**

The Bettmann Archive — 42

Historical Pictures Service — 11 (bottom), 14, 17
(2 pictures), 19 (4 pictures), 20, 22, 23, 26, 28,
34, 36, 37, 38, 39, 41, 47, 52, 54, 57, 59, 61, 62,
63, 65, 67 (2 pictures), 70, 76, 79, 82, 84, 85

Courtesy Library of Congress — 4, 25, 27, 29, 31,
35, 45, 46, 56, 66, 68, 86

Nawrocki Stock Photo — 5, 9, 11 (top), 40, 53,
73, 75 (2 pictures)

H. Armstrong Roberts — 6, 24, 32, 48

U.S. Bureau of Printing and Engraving — 2

Vision Quest — 80

Cover design and illustration by
Steven Gaston Dobson

Childrens Press®, Chicago
Copyright ©1987 by Regensteiner Publishing Enterprises, Inc.
All rights reserved. Published simultaneously in Canada.
Printed in the United States of America.

   10 11 12 13 14 15 16 17 R 02 01 00 99

A coin commemorating Martin Van Buren's inauguration in 1837

## Table of Contents

# Chapter 1

# The Panic of 1837

On Friday, February 10, 1837—less than a month before Martin Van Buren was sworn in as the eighth president of the United States—signs began to appear on building walls in New York City:

BREAD! MEAT! RENT! FUEL!
Their Prices Must Come Down!
*The voice of the people shall be heard and will prevail.*
The people will meet in the park, *rain or shine*, at
4 o'clock Monday Afternoon.

On Monday afternoon, thousands of New Yorkers gathered in a snow-covered Manhattan park to hear speakers from the Equal Rights party who had organized the mass meeting. Many of the listeners were poor and desperately hungry. At the time, America was plunging into a serious depression.

A number of events had brought on this economic decline. President Andrew Jackson, whom Van Buren served as vice-president, had recently demanded that people use gold or silver, instead of paper money, to buy land.

Americans were moving west, and suddenly western lands had to be bought with hard currency rather than bank notes. As gold and silver moved west to pay for new lands, money in the East became scarce. Also, crops over much of the U.S. had failed. Food prices doubled, and many people had little money to pay for food and shelter.

At the noisy meeting in New York, speakers complained that the price of wheat had gone from $8 a barrel to $15 in just a few days. Many New Yorkers found it impossible to buy flour to make bread. One of the speakers decided to attack a grain seller, Eli Hart, directly.

"Fellow citizens," he said to the angry crowd, "Mr. Hart has 53 barrels of flour in his stores. Let us go and offer him $8 a barrel, and if he does not take it . . . " Another man tapped the speaker on his shoulder and warned him not to finish the sentence by calling for violence. "And if he does not take it," the speaker concluded, "we will depart in peace." But the speaker snarled his final words as if to suggest he had something else in mind.

Immediately, a large group of people broke away from the crowd and marched down Broadway toward the Hart warehouse. They broke through the building's iron doors and forced their way inside. Before Eli Hart and a group of policemen arrived to stop them, the marchers had rolled thirty barrels of flour out onto the street.

The mayor of New York City rushed to the warehouse and tried to calm the crowd. As he spoke, hundreds of other people arrived from the park and began pelting him with snowballs. Once the mayor and the police were chased away, there was nothing to stop the angry mob.

**A cartoon showing Andrew Jackson fighting the "bank war" before the Panic of 1837**

The crowd of hungry people raced into Hart's warehouse and began throwing barrels of flour out of the upper windows. Six hundred barrels were sent flying, each one exploding like a bomb when it hit the pavement below. Before long, the street in front of Hart's warehouse was knee-deep in wheat and flour.

The police returned in force and fired muskets directly into the crowd. Despite the hazards, many men and women risked death to wade into the ocean of grain and fill their aprons and baskets with flour. In the meantime, other rioters had moved on to another warehouse. At the S. H. Herrick & Company building, fewer than a hundred barrels were thrown to the street before the entire New York City police department, along with soldiers from the U.S. Army, arrived to battle the mob.

Some of the rioters were captured and sentenced to long prison terms. In one sense, they were the lucky ones. At least in jail, they were fed and kept warm. Many of the rioters who escaped from the police later starved or froze to death on the streets of Manhattan.

Two weeks before his inauguration, President-Elect Martin Van Buren read about the riot and its sad aftermath in the Washington newspapers. He knew that the young nation was entering a period of desperate financial trouble. Some of the blame could be placed on the popular president he was replacing. Andrew Jackson, confined to bed in the White House because of illness, had changed the banking policies of the nation.

Because he felt that the huge Bank of the United States was more interested in helping the rich become richer than in serving common Americans, President Jackson had ended the power of the bank.

Smaller banks sprang up to take the place of the national bank, but many of them were not run wisely. Some offered so much credit based on paper money that the American economy was thrown into chaos.

The smaller banks were happy to loan people large amounts of money. Americans by the thousands borrowed paper money to buy land in the West and to build factories, farms, and steamboats.

Before long, so much paper money had flooded the economy that prices for goods and services began to rise. This situation, called inflation, was a serious problem in the final years of President Jackson's administration. It continued into Van Buren's term.

Political cartoons on Jackson's war with the Bank of the United States

In 1836, President Jackson decided to try to battle inflation by no longer allowing land to be purchased with paper money. Instead, those who wished to buy land in the American West would have to pay for it with gold or silver. But banks were not as ready and willing to make loans with hard currency as they had been with paper money. This affected businesses all over the country.

During the months that followed, thousands of banks and businesses failed. Foreign nations, especially England, grew alarmed and demanded immediate repayment of loans that they had made to the U.S. government. Before Van Buren had been in office for three months, about nine out of every ten factories in the eastern United States had closed their doors.

As a result, streets of eastern cities were filled with homeless people. Without jobs and without money to pay rent, they had been forced out of their homes and often huddled together in doorways and alleys to stay warm during the chilly hours of the summer night. By the following winter, many froze to death.

By the summer of 1837, just a few months after Van Buren had been in office, America was deep in the grip of its first great depression. Called the Panic of 1837, the depression lasted about five years, throughout the troubled administration of America's eighth president.

The man who led the nation through one of its most difficult times was a skilled politician. He had experience in the New York state government, in the U.S. Senate, and as vice-president for four years under the popular war hero Andrew Jackson.

Martin Van Buren's skill as a politician was vastly different than the skills of other presidents before him. Presidents such as George Washington and Andrew Jackson were famous soldiers. Others, such as Thomas Jefferson and John Adams, were known for their scholarship and writing ability.

But Martin Van Buren was neither a soldier nor a scholar. He had received only a few years of education at a small country school in Kinderhook, New York. He was not a great speaker and was not able to sway large audiences with his words.

However, Van Buren was the first president whose greatest skill was setting up and running political organizations behind the scenes. First in his native New York State and then in Washington, D.C., he built political organizations that continued for decades. His greatest efforts were made not on the floor of Congress but in the hallways and back rooms where he wheeled and dealed much like a modern politician.

Van Buren's skills at political organization earned him many nicknames, including the "Red Fox" and the "Little Magician."

Another nickname, because of his birth in Kinderhook, New York, was "Old Kinderhook." It is said that the initials for that name gave rise to the American expression "O.K." However, as he took office as the eighth president of the United States on March 4, 1837, the American economy was hardly O.K. Despite the political bag of tricks the "Little Magician" had developed, he had only a few weapons to fight the serious depression.

Martin Van Buren's birthplace in Kinderhook, New York

# Chapter 2

# Born under the
# American Flag

Martin Van Buren was born on December 5, 1782, in the little town of Kinderhook. The town, located near the eastern bank of the Hudson River in New York State, had been settled almost exclusively by Dutch families who had emigrated to America.

On the day Martin Van Buren was born, General George Washington was stationed in the town of Newburgh, about sixty miles down the Hudson River. The American Revolutionary War had just ended, and Washington and many of his soldiers were awaiting word from peace negotiators in Great Britain. Although a peace treaty was not signed until September 1783, Martin Van Buren would proudly point out years later that he was the first president to be born under the flag of the United States of America.

Kinderhook was unusual for a northern town. Slavery had been oulawed in New York soon after the revolutionary war, but the practice was continued somewhat secretly in the little Dutch town until well into the 1820s. Abraham Van Buren, Martin's father, owned six slaves at the time of Martin's birth.

The town's isolated location was one of the reasons that slavery continued to exist there. Although Kinderhook was just twenty miles south of Albany along the Hudson River, steamboats were still two decades away. Most people traveled overland on horseback or in stagecoaches. Few travelers between Albany and New York City stopped in the little Dutch town.

Years after Van Buren was born, the writer Washington Irving visited Kinderhook and used the town as the model for his famous story "The Legend of Sleepy Hollow." Irving wrote that the town was "one of the quietest places in the whole world," and that a "drowsy, dreamy influence" blanketed the whole region. The central character of the story, Ichabod Crane, visited "old Dutch wives, as they sat spinning by the fire, with a row of apples roasting and sputtering along the hearth." According to the story, Ichabod Crane listened to "their marvelous tales of ghosts and goblins, and haunted fields and haunted brooks."

While Kinderhook may have been an isolated, sleepy town, the Van Buren home was seldom without visitors. Abraham Van Buren, Martin's father, ran a tavern in the family home. Food and drink were served to many people traveling by stagecoach on the New York and Albany Post Road, which ran right by the Van Buren home.

Taverns, such as the one run by Abraham Van Buren, also served as hotels for travelers. Two well-known taverns in the 1700s were Lamb Tavern in Boston (above) and Suter's Tavern in Georgetown, near Washington, D.C. (right).

The one-and-a-half-story farmhouse must have been a lively place. It was crowded with Abraham and his wife Maria, eight children, six slaves, and the paying customers of the tavern. At their dinner table, the Van Burens spoke Dutch, as did most of the families in Kinderhook. In the large, first-floor room that was turned into a tavern, the visitors spoke English. Little Mat, as Martin was called, listened to the lively conversations of lawyers traveling between New York and Albany. Among the visitors to the Van Buren tavern were famous American politicians such as Alexander Hamilton, Aaron Burr, and John Jay, who became governor of New York in 1795.

When elections were held, the tavern was used as a polling place. Wealthy lawyers from Albany and even New York City often came to the tavern during elections to watch over the voting. The lawyers and politicians who traveled through Kinderhook made a lasting impression on young Mat. On official business of the young government, they dressed magnificently. With cocked hats set atop their powdered white wigs, the men wore deeply colored coats and velvet pants, silk stockings and silver buckles on their square-toed shoes.

Undoubtedly, Martin's greatest education came from the conversations he overheard in the tavern run by his family. He was fortunate to have such informal schooling, because he had little formal education. Although the Van Buren family farmed the land around their home, operated a tavern, and owned six slaves, they were far from wealthy. As soon as the children were old enough to work, they were expected to pitch in and help.

Above, left to right: Political leaders John Jay, Aaron Burr, and Alexander Hamilton. All three men were visitors to the Van Buren tavern at one time.

Right: Some examples of men's clothing fashions during Van Buren's time

An eighteenth-century schoolroom

With so much work to do around the house, Martin only occasionally attended the Kinderhook Academy, the little school in town. Built at the foot of a hill, the schoolhouse was so poorly lighted that students could barely read their books. Although Van Buren learned to read and write English and some Latin at the school, many people would say years later that his language skills were poor.

This fact haunted Van Buren throughout his life. Even though he rose in politics to hold the most important job in America, Van Buren often felt inferior to people who were better educated. "How often have I felt the necessity of a regular course of reading," he wrote after he was president, "to sustain me in my conflicts with able and better educated men."

In 1796, when he was only fourteen years old, Martin Van Buren's school days were over. In the early fall of that year, Martin left home to become an apprentice to the lawyer Francis Silvester. An apprentice worked for extremely low wages in order to learn a profession or trade. With Silvester, Martin swept the office floor, kept a fire burning in the stove, copied legal notes in longhand, and began learning the legal profession.

The same year that Martin became an apprentice, George Washington was completing his second term as the president of the United States. Although many people hoped that Washington would run for a third term, he refused. The president was deeply saddened that many of his advisers were arguing with each other. These men, like many people all over the young nation, seemed to be separating into opposing political parties.

Some people, such as Vice-President John Adams, were called Federalists and believed in a strong central government and in policies that helped wealthy merchants and manufacturers. The leader of the opposing Anti-Federalists was Secretary of State Thomas Jefferson. He and his followers distrusted a strong central government. They believed that average American citizens, not just wealthy businessmen, should help run their government. The Anti-Federalists soon became known as the Republican, or Democratic-Republican, party. (The names are confusing, because the Republican party of Van Buren's day became our present Democratic party.) Like many wealthy Americans, the members of the Silvester family were firm Federalists.

**Federalist John Adams**

Francis Silvester's father was a New York State senator. A little less than two years after Martin joined the Silvester family as an apprentice, the father ran again for the state senate as a Federalist and won. To celebrate the victory, many people in Kinderhook staged a giant festival where they fired a cannon and danced and dined through much of the night. The fifteen-year-old Martin refused to join the celebration and instead returned to his room and crawled into bed.

**Democratic-Republican Thomas Jefferson**

When Francis Silvester's brother Cornelius discovered Martin in bed and asked what was wrong, Van Buren explained that his own father believed in the Anti-Federalist policies of Thomas Jefferson, not in the policies of the Federalists. Even as a young man, Martin agreed with the Republicans. For more than an hour Cornelius tried unsuccessfully to talk Van Buren into becoming a Federalist.

Van Buren stayed with the Silvesters for five years but was never persuaded to change his beliefs. The experience did much to shape his personality. Even when he disagreed strongly with other people, Van Buren learned to be charming and pleasant. There was no point in a young apprentice angering his employers.

**Martin Van Buren before he became president**

In many other ways, however, he adopted the manners and tastes of the wealthy Silvesters. When he first came to work for the family, he was dressed so poorly that Francis asked him to buy new clothes. Before long, he was wearing the same kind of well-tailored outfits as his masters. Although he grew to be only five feet six inches tall, his curly blond hair, handsome face, and elegant clothes made a striking appearance—so much so, that some people criticized him as a dandy.

Despite the social skills he had learned, Van Buren felt out of place as a young Republican living with a Federalist family. Before long, he began planning his escape.

24

New York's old City Hall, located on Wall Street

He developed a friendship with John P. Van Ness, leader of the Republican party in Kinderhook, as well as other members of the Van Ness family. The Van Nesses helped him become a delegate to a Republican party meeting held in nearby Troy in 1801. The same year, Van Buren worked hard campaigning for John P. Van Ness, who won a seat in the U.S. House of Representatives.

To express his thanks, Van Ness loaned Martin enough money to move south to New York City. There, Van Buren was given a job in the law firm of Van Ness's brother, William. For the first time in his life, Martin lived away from Kinderhook.

Aaron Burr shoots Alexander Hamilton in a duel.

The time he spent in New York City was relatively uneventful. Working closely with William Van Ness, he learned enough about the law in just two years to become a lawyer himself in November 1803. Almost immediately, he left William Van Ness's firm to return to Kinderhook to practice law.

It proved to be a wise move. Eight months later, Van Ness acted as the second (a kind of assistant) for Aaron Burr when Burr killed Alexander Hamilton in a duel. At the time, Burr was the vice-president of the United States under Thomas Jefferson. The vice-president was soon accused of murder, and Van Ness was accused of a crime for helping him.

**Hannah Hoes Van Buren**

Now a lawyer, Van Buren traveled back to New York City to defend his former employer in court. He proved his abilities by getting Van Ness released, in the process even calling in the governor of New York to help. By the time he went back to Kinderhook, Van Buren was becoming well known as a skilled lawyer.

After practicing law for only a few years in Kinderhook, Martin became so successful that he began to think about settling down and having a family. In February 1807, he married Hannah Hoes, a young lady from a Dutch family that had lived for several generations in Kinderhook. As Martin Van Buren settled into his first months of married life, great changes were in store for Kinderhook, for New York, and for much of the world.

**Robert Fulton's steamboat the *Clermont***

On August 17, 1807, Robert Fulton began the maiden voyage of his new steamboat, the *Clermont*. Though it was not the first steamship ever built, the *Clermont* was the first one to operate successfully. "Fulton's Folly," as the ship was first called, set out from New York City and sailed up the Hudson River, passing Kinderhook and arriving in Albany just thirty-two hours after it had left New York. The following year, Fulton built a great new steamship, the *Paragon*, that made the trip even faster.

**Graceful sailing ships in the Philadelphia harbor**

Practically overnight, the sleepy town of Kinderhook found itself next to a great highway—the Hudson River. Great steamships, powered by fire and steam, were changing Kinderhook and the world. Until 1807, few people ever bothered to travel on rivers, and the boats generally traveled only downstream. Now it was possible to carry heavy loads of raw materials and passengers upstream or downstream with relative ease. Great factories sprang up in Kinderhook and other towns along the Hudson. The new steamships made it easy for clothmakers, ironworkers, tailors, and farmers to send goods north to Albany or south toward New York City.

By the thousands, people came to Van Buren's Columbia County to live and work. The economy of Kinderhook and much of the rest of the state of New York grew wildly. In 1799, only three banks had existed in the entire state of New York. By 1812, when the age of the steamship was at hand, there were twenty banks serving the state.

In the booming economy of New York, Van Buren's legal practice flourished. He argued often at the New York Supreme Court in Albany, many times defending the rights of poor tenants against wealthy landlords.

Some of the rich Federalists in Kinderhook were angered by the little lawyer who "would neither worship at the shrine of wealth nor court the favor of the powerful." But Van Buren did not defend people simply because they were poor. When he felt that wealthy landowners were being wronged, he also helped to evict tenants from their land.

In 1812, at the age of thirty, Van Buren decided to embark on a political career. After helping other politicians win office, he decided to run for the office of New York State senator. Using his reputation as a defender of the common people, he was selected as the Republican senatorial candidate over two opponents. Now he had to run against the Federalist Edward P. Livingston, the grandson of a signer of the Declaration of Independence.

In the early 1800s, it took days and sometimes even weeks to collect and count votes. By the end of April, it appeared that Livingston had won. While some of the Federalists in Kinderhook laughed at him, Van Buren sadly boarded a steamship bound for New York City.

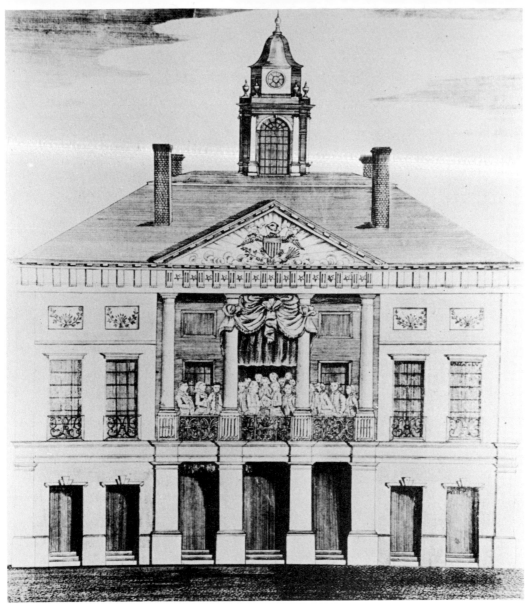

Federal Hall in New York City, the nation's capital from 1785 to 1790

A few miles downstream, however, a rowboat pulled up to the steamship and someone on the little boat announced that Van Buren had won. At twenty-nine, he was the second-youngest state senator in New York's history. For the career of the young lawyer, as well as for the young nation, it was full steam ahead.

# Chapter 3

# The New Politician

Martin Van Buren entered the New York State senate in the year 1812. It was a stormy time both for America and for the state of New York.

For some years prior to 1812, the emperor of France, Napoleon Bonaparte, had been fighting other European nations, especially Great Britain. America's third president, Thomas Jefferson, had tried desperately to keep his country out of these European wars. Despite his efforts, a number of American ships were attacked by British naval vessels, whose commanders wanted Americans to stop all trade with France.

By early 1812, a number of U.S. congressmen were calling for open war against Great Britain. Within a few months, these congressional "war hawks" had their way. Congress declared war on Great Britain on June 18, 1812. Less than two months after Van Buren was elected to his first political office, the War of 1812 had begun.

Opposite page: An engraving
of Martin Van Buren

**Francis Scott Key, who wrote "The Star-Spangled Banner"**

The conflict lasted only about two and one-half years, but a number of important events occurred during this relatively short time. In the summer of 1814, British troops invaded Washington, D.C., burned the White House and the Capitol, and marched on Baltimore. It was during their unsuccessful attempt to capture Baltimore that Francis Scott Key wrote "The Star-Spangled Banner." The final battle of the war—the Battle of New Orleans—was fought at the mouth of the Mississippi River, where the American general Andrew Jackson soundly defeated the British troops.

**Andrew Jackson (right) at the Battle of New Orleans**

For a number of young American politicians, who lived their lives for the most part between the revolutionary war and the Civil War, the War of 1812 was their greatest test. It was especially so for Van Buren, since a number of the war's largest battles were fought in and around New York. The state's legislature faced many challenges brought on by the fighting.

In 1812, Van Buren had called for "war, and war alone" against Great Britain. He wanted an all-out struggle against the nation that had "sought to strangle us in our infancy." He wrote a paper for other Republican politicians in New York in which he called Americans "the only free people on earth" and America "the last republic." He warned that European leaders believed that republics could "never stand the rude shock of war."

**The American victory at the Battle of Lake Champlain**

Although he advocated war and did all he could to support it in the New York legislature, Van Buren turned down an offer to become an officer in the American army. Years later, when Van Buren was Andrew Jackson's vice-president, the frontiersman Davy Crockett made fun of him for not joining in the battles of the War of 1812.

Instead as a legislator, Van Buren chose to work hard to ensure that New York could defend itself from British attacks. In his first year in the state senate, he wrote a bill that allowed the New York militia to draft twelve thousand "free white males, eighteen to forty-five, for a period of two years." The bill quickly passed the state legislature and became law. One of the last great battles of the war, the Battle of Lake Champlain, was fought late in 1814 in New York. By 1815, the war was over.

**New York City in 1822**

That year was a memorable one for Van Buren as well. A little more than two years after he began working in the New York State senate, he was appointed state attorney general. The attorney general was responsible for seeing that as many New Yorkers as possible obeyed the laws of the state. Being attorney general and state senator at the same time helped Van Buren increase his political power.

Van Buren had a number of achievements during his first term in the New York senate. One of the most significant was his proposal to abolish debtors' prisons. In the early nineteenth century, people who were unable to pay their bills were often put into prison. Van Buren thought it was unfair to punish people merely for being poor. He was one of the first lawmakers in America to introduce a bill against debtors' prisons. Also during his first term, he helped to rewrite the New York State constitution.

New York harbor and docks, as seen from Brooklyn in 1820

With the War of 1812 finally at an end, Americans began to think more about improving inland waterways for steamboat travel. For several years, some New Yorkers had dreamed about building a canal that would link the Hudson River with the Great Lakes. Plans for this waterway, which became known as the Erie Canal, had been made as early as 1783, soon after the revolutionary war. Some work had been done on the canal in the decades after the revolution. Once the War of 1812 ended, people began to think seriously about completing it.

**The construction of the Erie Canal**

In 1816, a bill for finishing the Erie Canal was proposed in the New York senate. As a Republican, Van Buren found it difficult to support a huge project that might well need federal funds to be completed. At the same time, he realized that many New Yorkers were strongly in favor of the canal's construction. A new waterway could open up vast areas of land in upstate New York and around the Great Lakes.

As he often did when he had to take an unpopular stand, Van Buren tried to disguise his actions. Already the most influential Republican in the state senate, he managed to have the wording that allowed the start of construction removed from the canal bill. At the same time, he put in new wording that called for more studies of the waterway.

**The lock gates of the Erie Canal at Lockport, New York**

The following year, however, Van Buren had a dramatic change of mind. Construction of the canal, he said, would "raise the state to the highest possible pitch of fame and grandeur." His speech in the state senate, and his hard work talking with legislators in hallways and offices, persuaded five senators to vote for the canal instead of against it. Had it not been for Van Buren's support, the Erie Canal might never have been built. What led to his remarkable change of mind?

Van Buren claimed that he voted in favor of the canal because the value of real estate in New York had risen dramatically. This would allow the waterway to be built using state funds raised from only a tiny increase in property taxes. While this was surely part of the reason, there was a far more important explanation.

New York governor DeWitt Clinton

A Republican politician named DeWitt Clinton was running for governor of New York. Van Buren, no friend of Clinton's, backed other candidates for the governorship. Clinton was strongly in favor of building the Erie Canal, and many New Yorkers, especially those who lived upstate, agreed with him. Van Buren made his sudden switch to support the canal project just two days before the election. He probably did this to increase his own candidates' popularity.

Unlike most of the politicians who had lived through the revolutionary war, Van Buren proved that he was willing to put party politics ahead of his own beliefs. DeWitt Clinton won the election despite Van Buren's change of heart, but many people felt that it was Van Buren, not Clinton, who saved the canal.

An early locomotive system, running around the year 1848

The Erie Canal was completed seven years later. Until the coming of the railroads in the mid-1800s, it was one of the most vital links between the East Coast and the American West.

In spite of his early political successes, however, for Martin Van Buren, the year 1817 marked the beginning of the most unhappy era in his life.

For three long years, one tragedy after another struck him, both personally and politically. His father, Abraham, died in 1817. His mother, Maria, succumbed a year later. Hannah Van Buren, Martin's wife, had been suffering from tuberculosis since 1816. In 1817, she gave birth to her fourth son and never fully recovered her strength. For two years, she grew weaker and weaker, finally passing away in February 1819. In less than three years, Martin Van Buren lost his father, his mother, and his wife. He now had to turn to relatives to help care for his children, but he still had to spend time on household chores.

Problems in his political career were soon added to his personal woes. In July 1819, Governor DeWitt Clinton, still angry that Van Buren had opposed him when he ran for governor during the Erie Canal debate, decided to fire Van Buren as attorney general. In one quick stroke, Van Buren's public offices were cut in half.

Since Van Buren and Clinton were both Republicans, Clinton's actions prompted a political war within the party. Van Buren decided to form his own branch of the Republican party, which became known as the Bucktails. Many other politicians in New York State soon considered themselves Bucktails. As one of their main goals, the Bucktails tried to undermine the Republican governor of New York, DeWitt Clinton.

Van Buren used what is now a familiar political method to gain control of the New York State legislature for his branch of the party. That method is called patronage, a system in which someone in political power can hire or fire whomever they wish. Van Buren was one of the earliest masters of the patronage system, which works today much like it worked in the early 1800s.

He used patronage to great advantage during the Erie Canal project. In 1819 and 1820, when work on the canal was progressing at a fever pitch, Van Buren managed to get a friend appointed to New York's state canal commission. Before long, he was able to control the commission.

Suddenly, Van Buren could decide who was hired and who was fired at the largest construction project in New York State history. A person who wanted a job, or who wanted to keep his job, working on the Erie Canal was expected to do favors for the Bucktails. Most favors involved voting for Bucktail candidates, contributing to their campaigns, and getting others to vote for Bucktails.

Trading jobs for political support is the foundation of the patronage system. While many people feel the system is not fair, patronage remains a fact of life in many local, state, and federal offices to this very day.

By 1820, Van Buren had used patronage to build a powerful political machine in New York State. The Bucktails also worked with a group of New York City politicians who had a political "machine," or organization, known as Tammany Hall. By developing friendships with the local politicians in New York City and the state politicians who belonged to the Bucktails in Albany, the capital, Van Buren was soon able to control much of the government of New York.

The Bucktails, led by Van Buren, were unable to keep DeWitt Clinton from being elected governor again in 1820. However, they gained nearly total control of the New York State legislature. By 1821, the Bucktails were able to fire many government workers who favored DeWitt Clinton. Hundreds of Bucktails replaced hundreds of Clintonian Republicans and Federalists in dozens of government offices. Martin Van Buren, fired as attorney general just a few years earlier, now virtually ran the New York State government.

**George Washington, first president of the United States**

The political machine Van Buren built ruled New York government for decades. In later years, the organization was known as the Albany Regency.

Compared to the lofty ideals of the Founding Fathers, Martin Van Buren's political machine seems less than a great achievement. George Washington had warned the nation against the formation of political parties. He seemed to feel that the country should be of a single mind and that parties were simply ways for selfish men to attain political power. Thomas Jefferson, confronted with the first truly bitter national election divided by party lines, tried to remove government workers from the opposing (Federalist) party only when he felt he had no choice.

Martin Van Buren's residence in Kinderhook, New York

On the other hand, Van Buren seemed to regard party feuding and the patronage system as facts of life. For better or worse, he was moving politics into a new era. Undoubtedly, his support for the party system was based partly on the success it brought him. But he also suggested that political parties gave the common people a way to participate in government. Parties gave the nation a kind of protection against influential individuals. "All men of sense know that political parties are inseparable from free governments," he once wrote.

**The south front of the White House in 1825**

The political machine Van Buren created gave him as much or more power in New York than he would have had as governor of the state. His ambitions soon turned to the national level, however. In 1821 he ran for the United States Senate and won.

As a senator, Van Buren would be leaving New York for Washington. It was his first great step toward the White House. From 1821 on, he was often absent from New York; but even from Washington, he managed to keep a watchful eye on his New York organization.

**Martin Van Buren**

# Chapter 4

# Senator, Governor, Secretary of State, Vice-President

Martin Van Buren arrived in Washington while Congress was in recess. Before he set foot on the floor of the U.S. Senate, he was already well known to the legislators in the nation's capital.

As the most powerful politician from the huge state of New York, Van Buren was an influential senator even before he began his federal career. From the outset, he mingled with members of high society in Washington, frequently going to dinner parties and the theater with other politicians and their families. Although not yet forty years old, Van Buren was a smashing success in the high society of the nation's capital.

His first speech as a U.S. Senator, however, got off to a rockier start. On February 12, 1822, the United States Senate was debating the issue of who owned a parcel of land in the state of Louisiana. For the nation as a whole, the debate was not a very important one. But for Martin Van Buren, the newly elected senator from New York, the issue provided him with an opportunity to give his first speech in the Senate.

As he rose from his chair to begin his talk, he grew frightened. He was not a great speaker, he knew, nor was he as well educated as many of the other senators. The usually calm politician began to panic. He started his speech by stuttering through the first few words.

As the other senators looked on with amusement, Van Buren finally stopped his attempts at speaking and returned to his chair. Many of the other senators must have wondered how this timid, awkward speaker could have gotten so much power in New York State politics. The answer came just a few minutes later.

Although deeply embarrassed, the young senator somehow managed to collect his thoughts. He rose again to speak, and this time he overcame his shyness. He spoke on the question of the Louisiana land claim for about two hours. If nothing else, Senator Van Buren proved that he could speak for just as long a time as any other senator.

Many people in Washington wondered if the senator from New York would decide to marry again. Van Buren often went to dances and the theater with Ellen Randolph, a granddaughter of Thomas Jefferson. When he traveled to Monticello, the home of the old president, people speculated it was to talk of marriage. Despite the rumors, Van Buren remained a widower for the rest of his life. He was far too busy with politics to consider a serious romance.

During his earliest years in the Senate, Van Buren began to take positions that would strengthen his political machine in New York State and increase his role as a national political leader. He immediately took an interest in federal employees assigned to work in his native state.

More importantly, from almost the first day he took his seat in the U.S. Senate, he began to think of national politics and the presidency, although not for himself at first. "I have seen enough of state politics for many years," he wrote to a friend. "I have made my debut here [in Washington] and am abundantly satisfied."

Although America's Civil War was still more than forty years away, many politicians were already arguing bitterly over the question of slavery. Senators and other politicians from the southern states believed that slavery was necessary. A growing number of northern politicians realized that slavery was immoral and wanted it outlawed throughout the country.

Although he was from the northern state of New York, where slavery was illegal, Martin Van Buren was technically a slaveholder. His single slave, a man named Tom, had run away eight years earlier. Van Buren, however, took few steps to find him.

In 1822, Van Buren's first full year in the Senate, the United States government was organizing the new territory called Florida. Throughout Congress, politicians argued over whether slavery should be allowed in the Territory of Florida. Van Buren helped to pass a law restricting slaves from being brought into Florida. The law also allowed slaves already in Florida to remain in slavery.

Van Buren hoped to please both northerners and southerners with his position. Northerners would be satisfied that he was against expanding legal slavery to new areas of the nation. He hoped to please southerners by allowing slavery to continue where it already existed.

**Presidential candidate William H. Crawford**

In 1824, Van Buren tried to help a man named William
Crawford become president of the United States. In order
to be nominated, Crawford had to defeat Andrew Jackson,
a hero of the War of 1812, and some other politicians as
well. Van Buren helped Crawford as much as he could, but
Crawford suffered a stroke that possibly cost him the
presidency. Jackson was not victorious either. It was John
Quincy Adams who won the election to become America's
sixth president.

**DeWitt Clinton unites Great Lakes and Atlantic Ocean waters at the opening of the Erie Canal.**

During the following year, 1825, New York's Erie Canal was finally completed. The New York State government, in large part controlled by Van Buren even though he spent a portion of each year in Washington, had spent $7 million on the project. The canal was actually an enormous, water-filled ditch, 363 miles long, 40 feet wide, and 4 feet deep. Boats that traveled on the Erie Canal were pulled by ropes tied to teams of horses that walked along the shore.

Travel on the canal was not very fast—about the speed at which a horse could walk. But for the first time, passengers and cargo could travel from New York City to the Great Lakes over water. Soon New York City overtook Philadelphia as the largest port in North America.

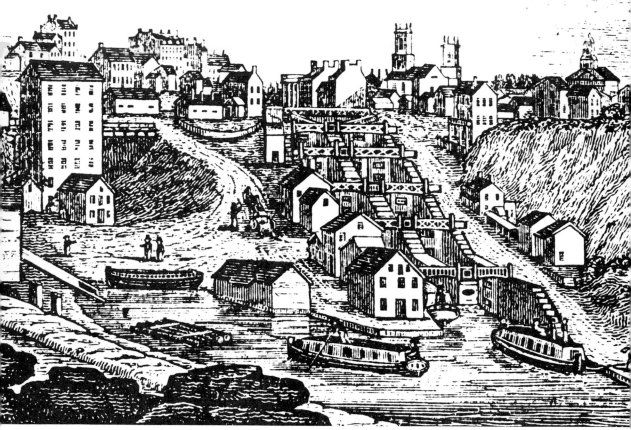

The system of locks on the Erie Canal enabled boats to travel uphill and down.

As the importance of the Erie Canal became clear, people in other regions of the country began to wonder how they could compete with it. The Cumberland Road was built over the southern Appalachian Mountains in hopes that it would offer another route for traveling west. The same year that the canal was completed, a new invention began making stagecoach travel much more pleasant. Specially curved steel springs were devised that took much of the jolt out of riding on bumpy dirt roads.

In just four more years, it was learned that a steam engine could successfully power a locomotive pulling railroad cars behind it. Over a period of several decades, the railroad gradually took over the business of moving people and supplies westward. In the early years after the completion of the Erie Canal, however, few Americans had ever heard of railroads. When the Baltimore & Ohio Railroad began to build the first tracks across a mountain range, a Pennsylvania newspaper editor asked, "What is a railroad? Perhaps some correspondent can tell us." Apparently, no one could.

Impressed by the success of the Erie Canal, many other states decided to build their own canals. More than a thousand miles of these waterways were built in the state of Pennsylvania alone.

During 1826 and 1827, Martin Van Buren continued to oppose legislation introduced in the Senate to build new roads and canals at federal expense. It was a convenient stand for Van Buren to take. The Republican party based many of its ideas on the philosophies of Thomas Jefferson. Jefferson, Van Buren gleefully pointed out, distrusted a strong central government and was opposed to spending federal dollars on improvements within the various states. At the same time, of course, his opposition to internal improvements helped to ensure the unchallenged importance of the Erie Canal.

The canal played a significant role in keeping his political machine in Albany operating smoothly. As always, Van Buren thought about the political side of every question he considered.

General Andrew Jackson

During the mid-1820s, the senator from New York began to support Andrew Jackson for the next presidential election in 1828. Working behind the scenes as always, Van Buren helped to organize many people to support General Jackson. But Martin Van Buren was not the kind of politician who left things to chance. His home state of New York, he knew, contained one-seventh of the population of the entire United States. It also could boast of the largest port in the New World—New York City—and the most important route in the nation for carrying goods from the eastern seaboard to the western frontier—the Erie Canal.

Van Buren decided to use his popularity in this powerful state to help elect Andrew Jackson president. He gave up his seat in the U.S. Senate and ran for governor of New

John Quincy Adams

York. For New Yorkers voting in the election of 1828, the names of Andrew Jackson and Martin Van Buren would appear near the top of the Democratic ballot. As the most popular politician in New York, Van Buren's name was sure to help Jackson.

Van Buren added a final, winning touch to this strategy. He and his helpers came up with a slogan to help Jackson defeat John Qunicy Adams, the incumbent president. They assured everyone who would listen that the election was between "John Quincy Adams, who can write, and Andrew Jackson, who can fight." It was all too much for the supporters of Adams. When the election was over, Andrew Jackson had won the presidency and Martin Van Buren was the governor-elect of the state of New York.

For the first time, Van Buren was the elected head of the New York political organization he had been running for years. He would no longer work in the Capitol Building in Washington part of each year. Now his full duties were in Albany, the capital of New York State, near the eastern end of the Erie Canal.

Surprisingly, he served as the governor of New York for less than three months. He was called back to Washington by the new president, Andrew Jackson. President Jackson was thankful for the help Van Buren had given him in his bid for the presidency. As a reward, Van Buren became Jackson's secretary of state, one of the most important members of the president's cabinet.

On a chilly evening in March 1829, Van Buren's stagecoach pulled up in front of a Washington hotel. As the new secretary of state stepped down onto the street, he was surrounded by a crowd of people. Almost all of them were men looking for jobs and important offices in the new government of Andrew Jackson. For some time, Van Buren was hounded day and night by people looking for positions in the new government.

Some historians claim that Van Buren was the first politician to bring patronage into the national government. Others have said that that statement is too strong. It is a fact that he fired many government workers who did not support Jackson's party. "We give no reasons for our removals," he once said coldly about firing people. Under the new Secretary of State Martin Van Buren, government workers soon learned that they had better support his party at all times or look for other jobs.

A "hickory pole" campaign parade for Andrew Jackson

Van Buren immediately became an important member of President Jackson's cabinet and part of a circle of unofficial advisers known as the "Kitchen Cabinet." President Jackson, who was called "Old Hickory," was a frontiersman who cared little about the complicated manners that concerned most world leaders. On the other hand, Van Buren had grown up among eastern lawyers and knew how to behave in society without angering people, even when there were serious disagreements. Thus, President Jackson could rely on Van Buren to meet with important foreign dignitaries.

As secretary of state, Van Buren gave valuable service to President Jackson and the United States. He negotiated trade agreements with the British in the West Indies and talked the Turkish government into allowing American ships to sail on the Black Sea. He also persuaded the French government to pay damages resulting from the Napoleonic Wars.

Considering his skill as secretary of state, it is surprising that Van Buren remained at the post for less than three years. He resigned before the end of Andrew Jackson's first term in office to help the president and to further his own career.

One of the other members of Jackson's cabinet was Secretary of War John Eaton. Shortly before he joined the cabinet, Eaton married a pretty young widow named Margaret.

Many people in Washington, including some members of Jackson's cabinet, believed that Margaret was an immoral woman. The president disagreed. Before long, Jackson's entire cabinet was arguing about whether Margaret Eaton was a well-behaved woman.

As was so often the case, Van Buren found a way to turn a delicate question to his own political advantage. He decided to help President Jackson defend the honor of Margaret Eaton.

While many members of Washington's high society snubbed her, Van Buren was careful to visit her often and to be polite to her on all occasions. Soon the cabinet was in an uproar. One of the men most critical of Margaret Eaton was Vice-President John Calhoun.

**A cartoon depicting Margaret Eaton being called before the cabinet**

Although Van Buren and President Jackson had become close friends, Van Buren decided to resign over what became known as "the Eaton Affair." He made it clear that he thought the whole thing was ridiculous and that it was ruining the government. Van Buren's resignation embarrassed everyone in the cabinet, as well as Vice-President Calhoun. Soon, the rest of the cabinet resigned as well. Jackson was able to appoint new advisers. Calhoun, a leading contender for the presidency after Jackson, never fully recovered from the embarrassment.

**Vice-President John C. Calhoun**

To reward him for his help, President Jackson appointed Van Buren to the post of minister to England. Van Buren sailed to London and made an extremely favorable impression on the government there. However, the U.S. Senate still had to approve the appointment. After some debate, the vote in the Senate was tied. Vice-President Calhoun cast the tie-breaking vote aginst Van Buren. "It will kill him, sir, kill him dead," the vice-president gleefully remarked about his vote against Van Buren. Just to make sure he made the point, he added, "He will never kick sir, never kick."

Senator Thomas Hart Benton had a ready answer. "You have broken a minister, and elected a Vice President," he said. He was right.

A "bank war" cartoon of 1834, in which Jackson takes on bank president Biddle

President Jackson ran for his second term in 1832. His relations with Vice-President Calhoun were so bad that Calhoun resigned from the ticket. Jackson then chose Martin Van Buren as his running mate.

In the campaign that followed, Jackson and Van Buren argued against the huge Bank of the United States. Both claimed that the bank was run to benefit wealthy individuals and businesses. Alarmed officials of the bank gave large "loans" to congressmen and other politicians who opposed the election of Jackson and Van Buren.

When the votes were counted, however, the two men had received a decisive majority. Jackson was elected to a second term and Martin Van Buren became the new vice-president of the United States.

The stagecoach of the vice-president-elect arrived in Washington on the last Tuesday in February 1833. The following Monday, Chief Justice John Marshall administered the oath of office to President Jackson and, minutes later, to Vice-President Van Buren.

The years of Martin Van Buren's vice-presidency were not easy ones. President Jackson was in poor health and was gravely ill throughout the first summer Van Buren was in office.

Although Jackson was often so ill he found it nearly impossible to get out of bed, he wasted little time trying to destroy the Bank of the United States.

Almost from the moment he took office, Van Buren was alarmed to discover that many of Jackson's advisers wanted to remove all federal money from the Bank of the United States immediately. Since the money would have to be put elsewhere, some of the advisers wanted Van Buren to select the banks that would be given the huge deposits.

For years, Van Buren had reached for greater and greater power by wheeling and dealing with other politicians away from the view of the public. Throughout his career, however, he had never been involved in a scandal over money.

If he were to choose what became known as "pet banks" to hold the money of the U.S. government, he could easily get himself in political trouble. His politician's instincts told him to stay away from the decision. It was left up to others, though this may have been a serious mistake. Many of the "pet banks" that were chosen invested their huge new funds unwisely.

An 1836 election cartoon, showing Henry Clay dueling Van Buren

By the final year of Andrew Jackson's presidency, the stage was set for the Panic of 1837. Arguments among Washington politicians grew so bitter that Van Buren kept two pistols hidden under his coat whenever he appeared in public. Nevertheless, Andrew Jackson remained a popular president. Few were willing to blame the president or the vice-president for the troubles that affected the nation.

With President Jackson's blessing, Martin Van Buren ran for president of the United States in 1836. Not everyone shared Jackson's good feelings toward the vice-president. William Seward, at the time a New York State senator, called Van Buren a "crawling reptile." Others pointed out that he seemed to care for nothing except power.

Andrew Jackson in his later years

Most people in the United States felt, however, that Van Buren stood for the same things that their beloved Andrew Jackson did. Van Buren would be like Jackson, they felt. He would stand up for the common man while other politicians merely helped the rich get richer.

Against a number of other candidates, especially an army general named William Henry Harrison, Van Buren won the election of 1836. In a few months, he would become the eighth president of the United States.

In the meantime, the American economy collapsed.

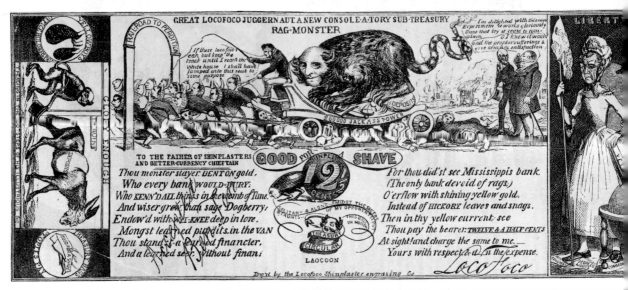

Above: A humorous
bank note printed in
1837, after Jackson's
war on the Bank of
the United States. Van
Buren, the creature
on the coach, was
believed to hold the
same political views as
Jackson.

Right: William Henry
Harrison, who was
defeated by Van
Buren in the 1836
presidential election

# Chapter 5

# Eighth President of the United States

On the morning of the first Saturday in March 1836, President-Elect Martin Van Buren rode in a horse-drawn carriage to the White House. The ailing Andrew Jackson was still living inside. Van Buren had insisted that the old president remain in the White House until he recovered his health.

Just before noon, Jackson joined the new president in a carriage made from wood taken from the famous American warship U.S.S. *Constitution*, nicknamed "Old Ironsides." Together, the outgoing president and the president-elect rode down Pennsylvania Avenue toward the Capitol Building. As the team of four gray horses pulled the carriage past the crowds lining Pennsylvania Avenue, Martin Van Buren tried his best to look cheerful. He was about to take the oath of office to become the eighth president of the United States. It should have been a happier day.

Van Buren inherits the problems of Jackson's administration.

However, less than a month earlier, hundreds of people had rioted in New York City over the high cost of food. In the large cities of America's East Coast, hard money was becoming extremely difficult to find. As each day passed, paper money purchased less and less. Many city dwellers already had trouble paying their rent, and the worst was yet to come. The country was entering the most serious economic crisis of its sixty-year history, and Van Buren would be president during this terrible time.

On Van Buren's inaugural day, however, the full scope of the disaster was not yet clear. As the carriage carrying the two presidents reached the steps of the Capitol Building, twenty thousand spectators cheered its arrival. The crowd parted as Van Buren and Jackson, followed by other officials, walked up the long Capitol stairway.

Van Buren delivered his inaugural address, then was sworn into office by the chief justice of the United States, Roger Taney. Strangely enough, no vice-president was sworn in on that day.

In Martin Van Buren's time, the president and the vice-president were elected separately. None of the candidates for vice-president had won a majority of the electoral votes, so the vote went to the Senate. Finally Van Buren's running mate, Richard M. Johnson, was chosen to be vice-president.

Much of the new president's inaugural address discussed slavery, an issue of growing significance in the United States. Van Buren called the institution of slavery one of the most important "sources of discord and disaster" facing the nation. In typical fashion, he refused to support or condemn it. Instead, he called for "calm and enlightened judgment" to govern "our people as one vast body." As he often did in the past, the new president once again refused to take a clear stand on a controversial issue. In the same speech, Van Buren stated that the American economy was "perfectly secured," that is, in sound condition. Within days, the statement was proved to be wildly inaccurate.

Before the end of March, the same month that the luckless new president came to office, New York businessmen knew they were facing disaster. Many banks did not have enough hard cash to meet the needs of their business and private customers. They issued paper credits, usually signed by a bank official; but little trust was placed in these bank notes.

By early May, New York City was in turmoil. Land at Broadway and 100th Street, in midtown Manhattan, had sold for nearly $500 per lot in 1835. By the first week of May in 1836, the same lots sold for $50—when a buyer with real money could be found.

On May 9, all the banks in New York City agreed to stop making payment in coins of the United States mint. There simply wasn't enough real money to go around. The banks offered paper credits instead, which soon became practically worthless.

"Where will it all end?" a wealthy New Yorker asked. "In ruin, revolution, perhaps civil war." In other large eastern cities, such as Boston and Philadelphia, the situation quickly grew as desperate. Poorhouses were filled to capacity with people who had lost their homes and apartments. People searched frantically for jobs, but few employers had money to offer them.

Soon, most of the stores, offices, and factories in America's largest cities began to shut down. The money needed to run these businesses had all been sent to the western frontier to buy land.

Some politicians pointed out that the Erie Canal, for so long a boon to the economy of New York, had really guided the nation into a desperate crisis. The people who had moved west along that watery route seemed to take all the hard currency with them.

By the beginning of April, less than a month after Van Buren took office, many politicians realized that the country was in serious trouble. They asked the new president to call a special session of Congress to deal with the crisis.

**New York City during the depression of 1837**

But Van Buren did nothing. The man whose political career had risen with the steam engine—this deft politician who powered smooth-running political machines—was suddenly frozen into inactivity.

By May, nearly every politician in the country was demanding an emergency meeting of Congress to deal with the Panic of 1837. On May 15, the already embattled president ordered a special session of Congress to begin on the first Monday in September. It was a surprisingly long time to wait. Although congressmen would need time to travel back to Washington, there was a more significant reason for the delay. It would give Van Buren a chance to think of a plan.

Although he acted slowly, the plan Van Buren eventually developed resulted in the greatest achievement of his presidency.

The plan, though sound, would take years to carry out. In the meantime, Van Buren had to serve as president for an increasingly dissatisfied nation.

Van Buren's plan was an extremely important one. He decided that Andrew Jackson had been right in criticizing the huge Bank of the United States. The bank had clearly been more interested in serving its wealthiest customers than in acting in the best interests of all Americans, regardless of their economic level.

On the other hand, Van Buren knew that Jackson (and he, himself) had blundered by trying to set up a number of smaller "pet banks" to handle the huge cash deposits of the U.S. government.

These banks invested their money in many different ways, often without thinking of the best interests of the country.

For several months, the president worked on a solution to the country's terrible financial problems. He gradually decided to continue backing the demand by Andrew Jackson to pay for western lands with gold and silver, the so-called hard-money policy.

More importantly, however, Van Buren decided that his government should withdraw its money from all banks. The second part of his plan was that an independent treasury should be established. He reasoned that an independent treasury would be free from the business pressures that led to the Panic of 1837.

Above: Democratic congressmen "whitewashing" Van Buren
Below: A cartoon showing Van Buren at the mercy of his critics

**An anti-Van Buren cartoon showing the country in ruins**

As President Van Buren slowly prepared his plan for the special session of Congress to be held in September, other pressures were building in various East Coast cities. In Boston, mass meetings were held, most highly critical of Van Buren. A wealthy Boston cotton trader told an angry crowd that "no other people were so abused, cheated, plundered, and trampled upon by their rulers as Americans."

In New York, members of a growing political party who called themselves Whigs attacked Van Buren's support for Jackson's hard-money policy. They suggested that his views were a "high-handed measure of tyranny," not unlike the attitudes that had cost an English king his head.

In all the great eastern cities, people by the thousands suffered severe hardship. Many found themselves without homes, jobs, or adequate food.

On Monday, September 4, 1837, the long-awaited special session of Congress finally began.

On the second day of the session, Van Buren had his son Abraham read a speech to the assembled congressmen. In it, the president noted that "all communities are apt to look to Government for far too much." He went on to say that it was not the business of government to make people wealthy, and he attacked an economic system based on paper money.

But Van Buren's call for an independent treasury went unnoticed by many congressmen.

Instead, many of the politicians attacked Van Buren's views against the Bank of the United States and paper money. Senator Henry Clay, a famous Whig politician, said: "It was paper money that carried us through the Revolution, established our liberties, and made us a free and independent people."

Clay put forth the view that Van Buren's plan was "cold and heartless" and that Americans were "a bleeding people." He added that it was impossible to separate government money from banks. The cause of the Panic of 1837, he concluded, was "a hard money Government and a paper money people."

Many of the congressmen agreed with Henry Clay's ideas. By the time the Panic Session, as this session of Congress became known, was over, no real action had been taken. On October 16, 1837, the House voted 120 to 106 against Van Buren's bill for an independent treasury. It would be several years before Congress would pass a similar bill.

By now, a growing number of Americans had turned against Van Buren and his Democratic party. In the November elections, Whig politicians triumphed in the northern and eastern states. In the assembly of New York, the president's own home state, Whigs won 101 out of 128 seats. The results in many other states were similar.

Just before midnight on November 22, a mob of about three hundred Whigs carried a heavy brass cannon in front of the White House. They fired the big gun and shouted insults at the increasingly unpopular president. The mob marched on to the house of each member of Van Buren's cabinet and continued the riotous demonstrations. The president suffered in silence, spending most of his time locked away in the White House.

Economic conditions in the eastern United States were bad enough, but within days President Van Buren had other things to worry about. Throughout the month of December, a group of Canadians near Toronto began revolting against the British rulers of Canada. On December 14, an American with the peculiar name of Rensselaer Van Rensselaer was named Commander of the Patriot Army by a group of Canadians. Almost immediately, Van Rensselaer and his Patriot Army of just twenty-eight soldiers invaded Navy Island in the Niagara River, a stone's throw from the Canadian border.

Three days later, there were eight hundred soldiers, many of them Americans, in the Patriot Army on Navy Island. Canadians had been gathering American volunteers to battle the British. They hoped to establish at least part of Canada as an independent nation.

**The British attack on the *Caroline* in the Niagara River**

On December 27, British forces began to shell Navy Island with cannon fire. Two nights later, the American steamship *Caroline* docked near the little town of Schlosser on the Niagara River in New York. The ship had been carrying troops and supplies to the Patriot Army on Navy Island. At around midnight, on December 29, several boats filled with British troops crossed the Niagara River from Canada. They quickly boarded the *Caroline* and began attacking its crew and passengers with muskets and swords. Many Americans aboard the ship were slaughtered. By morning, their mangled bodies could be seen floating down the Niagara River. Americans living in northern New York State shouted for revenge.

**General Winfield Scott**

In 1837, news traveled slowly. Ironically, Samuel Morse had invented the equipment for the telegraph earlier that very year, but the first public telegram would not be sent until nearly seven years later. President Martin Van Buren did not learn about the slaughter until January 6, 1838.

On that day, he received a letter, dated December 30, 1837, from the district attorney of Erie County, New York. The letter described the events aboard the *Caroline*. "Our whole frontier is in commotion," the district attorney wrote, "and I fear it will be difficult to restrain our citizens from revenging, by a resort to arms, this flagrant invasion of our territory."

Van Buren read the report with alarm, greatly upset by the attack on the *Caroline*. At the same time, he knew that an army of Americans attacking a foreign colonial government without the approval of the U.S. government was both ridiculous and illegal.

The following Monday, the president sent a special message to Congress, in which he included the reports of the attack on the *Caroline*. He also called for soldiers to be stationed along the Canadian border in New York State but took no further military action. Although many people in northern New York State were ready to go to war, Van Buren instructed the army to remain at peace.

Through his carefully worded messages, Van Buren avoided an unnecessary war with British troops in Canada. Met by the American army of General Winfield Scott, the Patriot Army on Navy Island disbanded. Van Rensselaer was arrested and eventually imprisoned for accepting a military post from a foreign government. In this instance, at least, Van Buren had acted quickly and wisely.

The economic hardships that followed the Panic of 1837 plagued the president for his remaining years in office. Conditions eased a bit after 1837 but hard times persisted. Although some Democratic politicians managed to win elections over Whigs, Van Buren could not help them very much from his weakened position.

Many Americans saw Van Buren as a fence sitter who straddled every important issue and could seldom make up his mind. Although a majority finally agreed that he handled the Canadian problem wisely, many also thought that he mishandled the issue of Texas.

The Battle of the Alamo

In 1836, the same year that Van Buren won the presidential election, Texans declared their independence from Mexico. The heroic defense of the Alamo and the final Battle of San Jacinto in which a Texan army defeated a larger Mexican army occurred the same year.

Soon afterward, Texas was recognized as an independent country by America, England, France, Holland, and Belgium. But the Republic of Texas had problems defending its citizens from attacks by Mexicans and Indians. Many Texans wanted to join the United States and many Americans were more than willing to accept them.

President Van Buren feared arguments over whether Texas should be a slave state or a free state if it were to join the Union. To avoid this heated controversy, he opposed allowing Texas to become a state.

In the final year of Van Buren's presidency, a bill setting up an independent treasury was finally passed. It would be some years before the independent treasury was made permanent. That same year, 1840, he helped pass a bill setting up a ten-hour workday for government employees.

Although he was born into a relatively poor family, over the years Van Buren developed a taste for elegant clothes, fancy meals, and expensive surroundings. With many Americans still suffering from a poor national economy, the Democratic president made an easy target as the elections of 1840 approached.

Some Whig politicians referred to the "rotten court of King Martin I." Others wondered how a politician who had come to power championing the cause of the common man could sleep at night in a bed once used by a French king.

One congressman accused Van Buren of using "gold-framed mirrors as big as a barn door to behold his plain Republican self."

The Whigs nominated William Henry Harrison, a well-known soldier, as their presidential candidate. Without a great deal of enthusiasm, the Democrats renominated Van Buren. Before long, a Whig politician noted that Van Buren preferred to drink imported French wine instead of American hard apple cider. The contest became known as the "hard cider campaign."

In this 1840 election cartoon, William Henry Harrison knocks the Democrats off balance. President Van Buren, at the top of the column, has the farthest to fall.

It wasn't much of a campaign. By the time the Whigs finished painting the president as a cruel, calculating politician who cared little about common folks, it was all but over. William Henry Harrison won 234 electoral votes to just 60 for Van Buren. In the cruelest blow of all, even New York State went to Harrison.

Harrison watches from the White House window as Van Buren leaves. The doorman is "Major Jack Downing." Downing was the pen name of Seba Smith, a man who wrote political satires on events of the time.

An 1848 campaign banner for the anti-slavery Free-Soil party. The party nominated Van Buren for president and Charles F. Adams (the son of John Quincy Adams) for vice-president. Van Buren's defeat marked the end of his political career.

# Chapter 6

# Old Kinderhook

Thomas Jefferson once said—and Martin Van Buren heartily agreed—that for a president, "the two happiest days of his life were those of his entrance upon the office and of his surrender of it." As he prepared to surrender the White House, Van Buren welcomed everyone into it, even Whig politicians who a few weeks earlier had been chanting the Whig cry, "Van is a used up man."

After William Henry Harrison took office, the ex-president returned to Kinderhook, New York, where he had spent his youth. There, he fared better than the sixty-eight-year-old Harrison. After just one month in office, the new president died, and Vice-President John Tyler became the tenth president of the United States.

Before Van Buren had even left office, the legislature of Missouri nominated him for president in the election of 1844, nearly four years in the future. Not yet sixty years old, "Old Kinderhook" hoped he might become president once more.

He left the large home he called Lindenwald in Kinderhook to tour the southern and western portions of the country, where he felt his support was weakest. There was plenty of time to campaign.

In 1844, on the eve of the campaign season, President Tyler asked Van Buren to become a justice of the United States Supreme Court.

This was a clever move by Tyler, but it was not clever enough to fool a master politician. Van Buren was gaining considerable support from Democrats to be their presidential candidate for 1844. If he were to join the Supreme Court, he would no longer be a threat to the Whigs. Van Buren turned down the appointment to continue seeking the Democratic nomination.

It didn't come. The greatest issue facing the nation at the time was whether to accept Texas into the Union. Texas law allowed slavery, and Van Buren was growing more and more opposed to the practice. He came out against the annexation of Texas and lost the nomination to James K. Polk, who was in favor of accepting Texas and Oregon. This move would maintain the balance of slave and free states. James Polk won the election of 1844, and Texas was admitted to the Union the following year, while Tyler was still president.

Still, the aging politician was not finished. In his old age, he gradually grew away from his fence-sitting stance on important issues and spoke out more and more strongly against slavery.

In 1848, the Democrats nominated a man named Lewis Cass, whose views on slavery were not acceptable to the abolitionists. A number of anti-slavery groups gathered together to form a new political group called the Free-Soil party. The Free-Soilers nominated Van Buren as their candidate for president.

As a third party, the Free-Soil organization had little chance to win the election, but Van Buren did surprisingly well. He received enough votes to take the election away from the Democratic candidate, but it was Zachary Taylor who won in the end.

Throughout the 1850s, Van Buren enjoyed the life of a retired president. The things he had accomplished, both good and bad, were rapidly being forgotten; but few people forgot that he had once been president of the United States. Van Buren spent some of his retirement time traveling in Europe and visiting the Dutch towns of his ancestors. For a time, he lived in Italy.

When he returned to the United States, Van Buren took up residence in his Lindenwald mansion in Kinderhook. There, he worried as the clouds of civil war began to gather over America.

In Van Buren's view, President Buchanan was at fault. He blamed Buchanan for not doing enough to help prevent a war. In his last years, firmly convinced that slavery could no longer exist in America, Van Buren did what he could to help the presidential campaign of Abraham Lincoln. Although Van Buren continued to hope for peace, hostilities between the North and South finally erupted into the Civil War in April 1860.

Martin Van Buren passed away on July 29, 1862, during the second year of the war. He spent his last days supporting Abraham Lincoln and hoping that the terrible struggle facing the nation would be short-lived.

He had discovered, at last, that there were no more fences to sit upon.

# Chronology of American History

(Shaded area covers events in Martin Van Buren's lifetime.)

**About A.D. 982**—Eric the Red, born in Norway, reaches Greenland in one of the first European voyages to North America.

**About 1000**—Leif Ericson (Eric the Red's son) leads what is thought to be the first European expedition to mainland North America; Leif probably lands in Canada.

**1492**—Christopher Columbus, seeking a sea route from Spain to the Far East, discovers the New World.

**1497**—John Cabot reaches Canada in the first English voyage to North America.

**1513**—Ponce de Léon explores Florida in search of the fabled Fountain of Youth.

**1519-1521**—Hernando Cortés of Spain conquers Mexico.

**1534**—French explorers led by Jacques Cartier enter the Gulf of St. Lawrence in Canada.

**1540**—Spanish explorer Francisco Coronado begins exploring the American Southwest, seeking the riches of the mythical Seven Cities of Cibola.

**1565**—St. Augustine, Florida, the first permanent European town in what is now the United States, is founded by the Spanish.

**1607**—Jamestown, Virginia, is founded, the first permanent English town in the present-day U.S.

**1608**—Frenchman Samuel de Champlain founds the village of Quebec, Canada.

**1609**—Henry Hudson explores the eastern coast of present-day U.S. for the Netherlands; the Dutch then claim parts of New York, New Jersey, Delaware, and Connecticut and name the area New Netherland.

**1619**—The English colonies' first shipment of black slaves arrives in Jamestown.

**1620**—English Pilgrims found Massachusetts' first permanent town at Plymouth.

**1621**—Massachusetts Pilgrims and Indians hold the famous first Thanksgiving feast in colonial America.

**1623**—Colonization of New Hampshire is begun by the English.

**1624**—Colonization of present-day New York State is begun by the Dutch at Fort Orange (Albany).

**1625**—The Dutch start building New Amsterdam (now New York City).

**1630**—The town of Boston, Massachusetts, is founded by the English Puritans.

**1633**—Colonization of Connecticut is begun by the English.

**1634**—Colonization of Maryland is begun by the English.

**1636**—Harvard, the colonies' first college, is founded in Massachusetts. Rhode Island colonization begins when Englishman Roger Williams founds Providence.

**1638**—Delaware colonization begins as Swedes build Fort Christina at present-day Wilmington.

**1640**—Stephen Daye of Cambridge, Massachusetts prints *The Bay Psalm Book*, the first English-language book published in what is now the U.S.

**1643**—Swedish settlers begin colonizing Pennsylvania.

**About 1650**—North Carolina is colonized by Virginia settlers.

**1660**—New Jersey colonization is begun by the Dutch at present-day Jersey City.

**1670**—South Carolina colonization is begun by the English near Charleston.

**1673**—Jacques Marquette and Louis Jolliet explore the upper Mississippi River for France.

**1682** — Philadelphia, Pennsylvania, is settled. La Salle explores Mississippi River all the way to its mouth in Louisiana and claims the whole Mississippi Valley for France.

**1693** — College of William and Mary is founded in Williamsburg, Virginia.

**1700** — Colonial population is about 250,000.

**1703** — Benjamin Franklin is born in Boston.

**1732** — George Washington, first president of the U.S., is born in Westmoreland County, Virginia.

**1733** — James Oglethorpe founds Savannah, Georgia; Georgia is established as the thirteenth colony.

**1735** — John Adams, second president of the U.S., is born in Braintree, Massachusetts.

**1737** — William Byrd founds Richmond, Virginia.

**1738** — British troops are sent to Georgia over border dispute with Spain.

**1739** — Black insurrection takes place in South Carolina.

**1740** — English Parliament passes act allowing naturalization of immigrants to American colonies after seven-year residence.

**1743** — Thomas Jefferson is born in Albemarle County, Virginia. Benjamin Franklin retires at age thirty-seven to devote himself to scientific inquiries and public service.

**1744** — King George's War begins; France joins war effort against England.

**1745** — During King George's War, France raids settlements in Maine and New York.

**1747** — Classes begin at Princeton College in New Jersey.

**1748** — The Treaty of Aix-la-Chapelle concludes King George's War.

**1749** — Parliament legally recognizes slavery in colonies and the inauguration of the plantation system in the South. George Washington becomes the surveyor for Culpepper County in Virginia.

**1750** — Thomas Walker passes through and names Cumberland Gap on his way toward Kentucky region. Colonial population is about 1,200,000.

**1751** — James Madison, fourth president of the U.S., is born in Port Conway, Virginia. English Parliament passes Currency Act, banning New England colonies from issuing paper money. George Washington travels to Barbados.

**1752** — Pennsylvania Hospital, the first general hospital in the colonies, is founded in Philadelphia. Benjamin Franklin uses a kite in a thunderstorm to demonstrate that lightning is a form of electricity.

**1753** — George Washington delivers command that the French withdraw from the Ohio River Valley; French disregard the demand. Colonial population is about 1,328,000.

**1754** — French and Indian War begins (extends to Europe as the Seven Years' War). Washington surrenders at Fort Necessity.

**1755** — French and Indians ambush Braddock. Washington becomes commander of Virginia troops.

**1756** — England declares war on France.

**1758** — James Monroe, fifth president of the U.S., is born in Westmoreland County, Virginia.

**1759** — Cherokee Indian war begins in southern colonies; hostilities extend to 1761. George Washington marries Martha Dandridge Custis.

**1760** — George III becomes king of England. Colonial population is about 1,600,000.

**1762** — England declares war on Spain.

**1763** — Treaty of Paris concludes the French and Indian War and the Seven Years' War. England gains Canada and most other French lands east of the Mississippi River.

**1764** — British pass the Sugar Act to gain tax money from the colonists. The issue of taxation without representation is first introduced in Boston. John Adams marries Abigail Smith.

**1765** — Stamp Act goes into effect in the colonies. Business virtually stops as almost all colonists refuse to use the stamps.

**1766** — British repeal the Stamp Act.

**1767**—John Quincy Adams, sixth president of the U.S. and son of second president John Adams, is born in Braintree, Massachusetts. Andrew Jackson, seventh president of the U.S., is born in Waxhaw settlement, South Carolina.

**1769**—Daniel Boone sights the Kentucky Territory.

**1770**—In the Boston Massacre, British soldiers kill five colonists and injure six. Townshend Acts are repealed, thus eliminating all duties on imports to the colonies except tea.

**1771**—Benjamin Franklin begins his autobiography, a work that he will never complete. The North Carolina assembly passes the "Bloody Act," which makes rioters guilty of treason.

**1772**—Samuel Adams rouses colonists to consider British threats to self-government.

**1773**—English Parliament passes the Tea Act. Colonists dressed as Mohawk Indians board British tea ships and toss 342 casks of tea into the water in what becomes known as the Boston Tea Party. William Henry Harrison is born in Charles City County, Virginia.

**1774**—British close the port of Boston to punish the city for the Boston Tea Party. First Continental Congress convenes in Philadelphia.

**1775**—American Revolution begins with battles of Lexington and Concord, Massachusetts. Second Continental Congress opens in Philadelphia. George Washington becomes commander-in-chief of the Continental army.

**1776**—Declaration of Independence is adopted on July 4.

**1777**—Congress adopts the American flag with thirteen stars and thirteen stripes. John Adams is sent to France to negotiate peace treaty.

**1778**—France declares war against Great Britain and becomes U.S. ally.

**1779**—British surrender to Americans at Vincennes. Thomas Jefferson is elected governor of Virginia. James Madison is elected to the Continental Congress.

**1780**—Benedict Arnold, first American traitor, defects to the British.

**1781**—Articles of Confederation go into effect. Cornwallis surrenders to George Washington at Yorktown, ending the American Revolution.

**1782**—American commissioners, including John Adams, sign peace treaty with British in Paris. Thomas Jefferson's wife, Martha, dies. Martin Van Buren is born in Kinderhook, New York.

**1784**—Zachary Taylor is born near Barboursville, Virginia.

**1785**—Congress adopts the dollar as the unit of currency. John Adams is made minister to Great Britain. Thomas Jefferson is appointed minister to France.

**1786**—Shays's Rebellion begins in Massachusetts.

**1787**—Constitutional Convention assembles in Philadelphia, with George Washington presiding; U.S. Constitution is adopted. Delaware, New Jersey, and Pennsylvania become states.

**1788**—Virginia, South Carolina, New York, Connecticut, New Hampshire, Maryland, and Massachusetts become states. U.S. Constitution is ratified. New York City is declared U.S. capital.

**1789**—Presidential electors elect George Washington and John Adams as first president and vice-president. Thomas Jefferson is appointed secretary of state. North Carolina becomes a state. French Revolution begins.

**1790**—Supreme Court meets for the first time. Rhode Island becomes a state. First national census in the U.S. counts 3,929,214 persons. John Tyler is born in Charles City County, Virginia.

**1791**—Vermont enters the Union. U.S. Bill of Rights, the first ten amendments to the Constitution, goes into effect. District of Columbia is established. James Buchanan is born in Stony Batter, Pennsylvania.

**1792**—Thomas Paine publishes *The Rights of Man.* Kentucky becomes a state. Two political parties are formed in the U.S., Federalist and Republican. Washington is elected to a second term, with Adams as vice-president.

**1793**—War between France and Britain begins; U.S. declares neutrality. Eli Whitney invents the cotton gin; cotton production and slave labor increase in the South.

**1794**—Eleventh Amendment to the Constitution is passed, limiting federal courts' power. "Whiskey Rebellion" in Pennsylvania protests federal whiskey tax. James Madison marries Dolley Payne Todd.

**1795**—George Washington signs the Jay Treaty with Great Britain. Treaty of San Lorenzo, between U.S. and Spain, settles Florida boundary and gives U.S. right to navigate the Mississippi. James Polk is born near Pineville, North Carolina.

**1796**—Tennessee enters the Union. Washington gives his Farewell Address, refusing a third presidential term. John Adams is elected president and Thomas Jefferson vice president.

**1797**—Adams recommends defense measures against possible war with France. Napoleon Bonaparte and his army march against Austrians in Italy. U.S. population is about 4,900,000.

**1798**—Washington is named commander-in-chief of the U.S. Army. Department of the Navy is created. Alien and Sedition Acts are passed. Napoleon's troops invade Egypt and Switzerland.

**1799**—George Washington dies at Mount Vernon, New York. James Monroe is elected governor of Virginia. French Revolution ends. Napoleon becomes ruler of France.

**1800**—Thomas Jefferson and Aaron Burr tie for president. U.S. capital is moved from Philadelphia to Washington, D.C. The White House is built as presidents' home. Spain returns Louisiana to France. Millard Fillmore is born in Locke, New York.

**1801**—After thirty-six ballots, House of Representatives elects Thomas Jefferson president, making Burr vice-president. James Madison is named secretary of state.

**1802**—Congress abolishes excise taxes. U.S. Military Academy is founded at West Point, New York.

**1803**—Ohio enters the Union. Louisiana Purchase treaty is signed with France, greatly expanding U.S. territory.

**1804**—Twelfth Amendment to the Constitution rules that president and vice-president be elected separately. Alexander Hamilton is killed by Vice-President Aaron Burr in a duel. Orleans Territory is established. Napoleon crowns himself emperor of France. Franklin Pierce is born in Hillsborough Lower Village, New Hampshire.

**1805**—Thomas Jefferson begins his second term as president. Lewis and Clark expedition reaches the Pacific Ocean.

**1806**—Coinage of silver dollars is stopped; resumes in 1836.

**1807**—Aaron Burr is acquitted in treason trial. Embargo Act closes U.S. ports to trade.

**1808**—James Madison is elected president. Congress outlaws importing slaves from Africa. Andrew Johnson is born in Raleigh, North Carolina.

**1809**—Abraham Lincoln is born near Hodgenville, Kentucky.

**1810**—U.S. population is 7,240,000.

**1811**—William Henry Harrison defeats Indians at Tippecanoe. Monroe is named secretary of state.

**1812**—Louisiana becomes a state. U.S. declares war on Britain (War of 1812). James Madison is reelected president. Napoleon invades Russia.

**1813**—British forces take Fort Niagara and Buffalo, New York.

**1814**—Francis Scott Key writes "The Star-Spangled Banner." British troops burn much of Washington, D.C., including the White House. Treaty of Ghent ends War of 1812. James Monroe becomes secretary of war.

**1815**—Napoleon meets his final defeat at Battle of Waterloo.

**1816**—James Monroe is elected president. Indiana becomes a state.

**1817**—Mississippi becomes a state. Construction on Erie Canal begins.

**1818**—Illinois enters the Union. The present thirteen-stripe flag is adopted. Border between U.S. and Canada is agreed upon.

**1819**—Alabama becomes a state. U.S. purchases Florida from Spain. Thomas Jefferson establishes the University of Virginia.

**1820**—James Monroe is reelected. In the Missouri Compromise, Maine enters the Union as a free (non-slave) state.

1821—Missouri enters the Union as a slave state. Santa Fe Trail opens the American Southwest. Mexico declares independence from Spain. Napoleon Bonaparte dies.

1822—U.S. recognizes Mexico and Colombia. Liberia in Africa is founded as a home for freed slaves. Ulysses S. Grant is born in Point Pleasant, Ohio. Rutherford B. Hayes is born in Delaware, Ohio.

1823—Monroe Doctrine closes North and South America to European colonizing or invasion.

1824—House of Representatives elects John Quincy Adams president when none of the four candidates wins a majority in national election. Mexico becomes a republic.

1825—Erie Canal is opened. U.S. population is 11,300,000.

1826—Thomas Jefferson and John Adams both die on July 4, the fiftieth anniversary of the Declaration of Independence.

1828—Andrew Jackson is elected president. Tariff of Abominations is passed, cutting imports.

1829—James Madison attends Virginia's constitutional convention. Slavery is abolished in Mexico. Chester A. Arthur is born in Fairfield, Vermont.

1830—Indian Removal Act to resettle Indians west of the Mississippi is approved.

1831—James Monroe dies in New York City. James A. Garfield is born in Orange, Ohio. Cyrus McCormick develops his reaper.

1832—Andrew Jackson, nominated by the new Democratic Party, is reelected president.

1833—Britain abolishes slavery in its colonies. Benjamin Harrison is born in North Bend, Ohio.

1835—Federal government becomes debt-free for the first time.

1836—Martin Van Buren becomes president. Texas wins independence from Mexico. Arkansas joins the Union. James Madison dies at Montpelier, Virginia.

1837—Michigan enters the Union. U.S. population is 15,900,000. Grover Cleveland is born in Caldwell, New Jersey.

1840—William Henry Harrison is elected president.

1841—President Harrison dies in Washington, D.C., one month after inauguration. Vice-President John Tyler succeeds him.

1843—William McKinley is born in Niles, Ohio.

1844—James Knox Polk is elected president. Samuel Morse sends first telegraphic message.

1845—Texas and Florida become states. Potato famine in Ireland causes massive emigration from Ireland to U.S. Andrew Jackson dies near Nashville, Tennessee.

1846—Iowa enters the Union. War with Mexico begins.

1847—U.S. captures Mexico City.

1848—John Quincy Adams dies in Washington, D.C. Zachary Taylor becomes president. Treaty of Guadalupe Hidalgo ends Mexico-U.S. war. Wisconsin becomes a state.

1849—James Polk dies in Nashville, Tennessee.

1850—President Taylor dies in Washington, D.C.; Vice-President Millard Fillmore succeeds him. California enters the Union, breaking tie between slave and free states.

1852—Franklin Pierce is elected president.

1853—Gadsden Purchase transfers Mexican territory to U.S.

1854—"War for Bleeding Kansas" is fought between slave and free states.

1855—Czar Nicholas I of Russia dies, succeeded by Alexander II.

1856—James Buchanan is elected president. In Massacre of Potawatomi Creek, Kansas-slavers are murdered by free-staters. Woodrow Wilson is born in Staunton, Virginia.

1857—William Howard Taft is born in Cincinnati, Ohio.

1858—Minnesota enters the Union. Theodore Roosevelt is born in New York City.

1859—Oregon becomes a state.

1860—Abraham Lincoln is elected president; South Carolina secedes from the Union in protest.

1861—Arkansas, Tennessee, North Carolina, and Virginia secede. Kansas enters the Union as a free state. Civil War begins.

1862—Union forces capture Fort Henry, Roanoke Island, Fort Donelson, Jacksonville, and New Orleans; Union armies are defeated at the battles of Bull Run and Fredericksburg. Martin Van Buren dies in Kinderhook, New York. John Tyler dies near Charles City, Virginia.

1863—Lincoln issues Emancipation Proclamation: all slaves held in rebelling territories are declared free. West Virginia becomes a state.

1864—Abraham Lincoln is reelected. Nevada becomes a state.

1865—Lincoln is assassinated in Washington, D.C., and succeeded by Andrew Johnson. U.S. Civil War ends on May 26. Thirteenth Amendment abolishes slavery. Warren G. Harding is born in Blooming Grove, Ohio.

1867—Nebraska becomes a state. U.S. buys Alaska from Russia for $7,200,000. Reconstruction Acts are passed.

1868—President Johnson is impeached for violating Tenure of Office Act, but is acquitted by Senate. Ulysses S. Grant is elected president. Fourteenth Amendment prohibits voting discrimination. James Buchanan dies in Lancaster, Pennsylvania.

1869—Franklin Pierce dies in Concord, New Hampshire.

1870—Fifteenth Amendment gives blacks the right to vote.

1872—Grant is reelected over Horace Greeley. General Amnesty Act pardons ex-Confederates. Calvin Coolidge is born in Plymouth Notch, Vermont.

1874—Millard Fillmore dies in Buffalo, New York. Herbert Hoover is born in West Branch, Iowa.

1875—Andrew Johnson dies in Carter's Station, Tennessee.

1876—Colorado enters the Union. "Custer's last stand": he and his men are massacred by Sioux Indians at Little Big Horn, Montana.

1877—Rutherford B. Hayes is elected president as all disputed votes are awarded to him.

1880—James A. Garfield is elected president.

1881—President Garfield is assassinated and dies in Elberon, New Jersey. Vice-President Chester A. Arthur succeeds him.

1882—U.S. bans Chinese immigration. Franklin D. Roosevelt is born in Hyde Park, New York.

1884—Grover Cleveland is elected president. Harry S. Truman is born in Lamar, Missouri.

1885—Ulysses S. Grant dies in Mount McGregor, New York.

1886—Statue of Liberty is dedicated. Chester A. Arthur dies in New York City.

1888—Benjamin Harrison is elected president.

1889—North Dakota, South Dakota, Washington, and Montana become states.

1890—Dwight D. Eisenhower is born in Denison, Texas. Idaho and Wyoming become states.

1892—Grover Cleveland is elected president.

1893—Rutherford B. Hayes dies in Fremont, Ohio.

1896—William McKinley is elected president. Utah becomes a state.

1898—U.S. declares war on Spain over Cuba.

1900—McKinley is reelected. Boxer Rebellion against foreigners in China begins.

1901—McKinley is assassinated by anarchist Leon Czolgosz in Buffalo, New York; Theodore Roosevelt becomes president. Benjamin Harrison dies in Indianapolis, Indiana.

1902—U.S. acquires perpetual control over Panama Canal.

1903—Alaskan frontier is settled.

1904—Russian-Japanese War breaks out. Theodore Roosevelt wins presidential election.

**1905**—Treaty of Portsmouth signed, ending Russian-Japanese War.

**1906**—U.S. troops occupy Cuba.

**1907**—President Roosevelt bars all Japanese immigration. Oklahoma enters the Union.

**1908**—William Howard Taft becomes president. Grover Cleveland dies in Princeton, New Jersey. Lyndon B. Johnson is born near Stonewall, Texas.

**1909**—NAACP is founded under W.E.B. DuBois

**1910**—China abolishes slavery.

**1911**—Chinese Revolution begins. Ronald Reagan is born in Tampico, Illinois.

**1912**—Woodrow Wilson is elected president. Arizona and New Mexico become states.

**1913**—Federal income tax is introduced in U.S. through the Sixteenth Amendment. Richard Nixon is born in Yorba Linda, California. Gerald Ford is born in Omaha, Nebraska.

**1914**—World War I begins.

**1915**—British liner *Lusitania* is sunk by German submarine.

**1916**—Wilson is reelected president.

**1917**—U.S. breaks diplomatic relations with Germany. Czar Nicholas of Russia abdicates as revolution begins. U.S. declares war on Austria-Hungary. John F. Kennedy is born in Brookline, Massachusetts.

**1918**—Wilson proclaims "Fourteen Points" as war aims. On November 11, armistice is signed between Allies and Germany.

**1919**—Eighteenth Amendment prohibits sale and manufacture of intoxicating liquors. Wilson presides over first League of Nations; wins Nobel Peace Prize. Theodore Roosevelt dies in Oyster Bay, New York.

**1920**—Nineteenth Amendment (women's suffrage) is passed. Warren Harding is elected president.

**1921**—Adolf Hitler's stormtroopers begin to terrorize political opponents.

**1922**—Irish Free State is established. Soviet states form USSR. Benito Mussolini forms Fascist government in Italy.

**1923**—President Harding dies in San Francisco, California; he is succeeded by Vice-President Calvin Coolidge.

**1924**—Coolidge is elected president. Woodrow Wilson dies in Washington, D.C. James Carter is born in Plains, Georgia. George Bush is born in Milton, Massachusetts.

**1925**—Hitler reorganizes Nazi Party and publishes first volume of *Mein Kampf.*

**1926**—Fascist youth organizations founded in Germany and Italy. Republic of Lebanon proclaimed.

**1927**—Stalin becomes Soviet dictator. Economic conference in Geneva attended by fifty-two nations.

**1928**—Herbert Hoover is elected president. U.S. and many other nations sign Kellogg-Briand pacts to outlaw war.

**1929**—Stock prices in New York crash on "Black Thursday"; the Great Depression begins.

**1930**—Bank of U.S. and its many branches close (most significant bank failure of the year). William Howard Taft dies in Washington, D.C.

**1931**—Emigration from U.S. exceeds immigration for first time as Depression deepens.

**1932**—Franklin D. Roosevelt wins presidential election in a Democratic landslide.

**1933**—First concentration camps are erected in Germany. U.S. recognizes USSR and resumes trade. Twenty-First Amendment repeals prohibition. Calvin Coolidge dies in Northampton, Massachusetts.

**1934**—Severe dust storms hit Plains states. President Roosevelt passes U.S. Social Security Act.

**1936**—Roosevelt is reelected. Spanish Civil War begins. Hitler and Mussolini form Rome-Berlin Axis.

**1937**—Roosevelt signs Neutrality Act.

**1938**—Roosevelt sends appeal to Hitler and Mussolini to settle European problems amicably.

**1939**—Germany takes over Czechoslovakia and invades Poland, starting World War II.

1940—Roosevelt is reelected for a third term.

1941—Japan bombs Pearl Harbor, U.S. declares war on Japan. Germany and Italy declare war on U.S.; U.S. then declares war on them.

1942—Allies agree not to make separate peace treaties with the enemies. U.S. government transfers more than 100,000 Nisei (Japanese-Americans) from west coast to inland concentration camps.

1943—Allied bombings of Germany begin.

1944—Roosevelt is reelected for a fourth term. Allied forces invade Normandy on D-Day.

1945—President Franklin D. Roosevelt dies in Warm Springs, Georgia; Vice-President Harry S. Truman succeeds him. Mussolini is killed; Hitler commits suicide. Germany surrenders. U.S. drops atomic bomb on Hiroshima; Japan surrenders: end of World War II.

1946—U.N. General Assembly holds its first session in London. Peace conference of twenty-one nations is held in Paris.

1947—Peace treaties are signed in Paris. "Cold War" is in full swing.

1948—U.S. passes Marshall Plan Act, providing $17 billion in aid for Europe. U.S. recognizes new nation of Israel. India and Pakistan become free of British rule. Truman is elected president.

1949—Republic of Eire is proclaimed in Dublin. Russia blocks land route access from Western Germany to Berlin; airlift begins. U.S., France, and Britain agree to merge their zones of occupation in West Germany. Apartheid program begins in South Africa.

1950—Riots in Johannesburg, South Africa, against apartheid. North Korea invades South Korea. U.N. forces land in South Korea and recapture Seoul.

1951—Twenty-Second Amendment limits president to two terms.

1952—Dwight D. Eisenhower resigns as supreme commander in Europe and is elected president.

1953—Stalin dies; struggle for power in Russia follows. Rosenbergs are executed for espionage.

1954—U.S. and Japan sign mutual defense agreement.

1955—Blacks in Montgomery, Alabama, boycott segregated bus lines.

1956—Eisenhower is reelected president. Soviet troops march into Hungary.

1957—U.S. agrees to withdraw ground forces from Japan. Russia launches first satellite, *Sputnik.*

1958—European Common Market comes into being. Fidel Castro begins war against Batista government in Cuba.

1959—Alaska becomes the forty-ninth state. Hawaii becomes fiftieth state. Castro becomes premier of Cuba. De Gaulle is proclaimed president of the Fifth Republic of France.

1960—Historic debates between Senator John F. Kennedy and Vice-President Richard Nixon are televised. Kennedy is elected president. Brezhnev becomes president of USSR.

1961—Berlin Wall is constructed. Kennedy and Khrushchev confer in Vienna. In Bay of Pigs incident, Cubans trained by CIA attempt to overthrow Castro.

1962—U.S. military council is established in South Vietnam.

1963—Riots and beatings by police and whites mark civil rights demonstrations in Birmingham, Alabama; 30,000 troops are called out, Martin Luther King, Jr., is arrested. Freedom marchers descend on Washington, D.C., to demonstrate. President Kennedy is assassinated in Dallas, Texas; Vice-President Lyndon B. Johnson is sworn in as president.

1964—U.S. aircraft bomb North Vietnam. Johnson is elected president. Herbert Hoover dies in New York City.

1965—U.S. combat troops arrive in South Vietnam.

1966—Thousands protest U.S. policy in Vietnam. National Guard quells race riots in Chicago.

1967—Six-Day War between Israel and Arab nations.

1968—Martin Luther King, Jr., is assassinated in Memphis, Tennessee. Senator Robert Kennedy is assassinated in Los Angeles. Riots and police brutality take place at Democratic National Convention in Chicago. Richard Nixon is elected president. Czechoslovakia is invaded by Soviet troops.

**1969**—Dwight D. Eisenhower dies in Washington, D.C. Hundreds of thousands of people in several U.S. cities demonstrate against Vietnam War.

**1970**—Four Vietnam War protesters are killed by National Guardsmen at Kent State University in Ohio.

**1971**—Twenty-Sixth Amendment allows eighteen-year-olds to vote.

**1972**—Nixon visits Communist China; is reelected president in near-record landslide. Watergate affair begins when five men are arrested in the Watergate hotel complex in Washington, D.C. Nixon announces resignations of aides Haldeman, Ehrlichman, and Dean and Attorney General Kleindienst as a result of Watergate-related charges. Harry S. Truman dies in Kansas City, Missouri.

**1973**—Vice-President Spiro Agnew resigns; Gerald Ford is named vice-president. Vietnam peace treaty is formally approved after nineteen months of negotiations. Lyndon B. Johnson dies in San Antonio, Texas.

**1974**—As a result of Watergate cover-up, impeachment is considered; Nixon resigns and Ford becomes president. Ford pardons Nixon and grants limited amnesty to Vietnam War draft evaders and military deserters.

**1975**—U.S. civilians are evacuated from Saigon, South Vietnam, as Communist forces complete takeover of South Vietnam.

**1976**—U.S. celebrates its Bicentennial. James Earl Carter becomes president.

**1977**—Carter pardons most Vietnam draft evaders, numbering some 10,000.

**1980**—Ronald Reagan is elected president.

**1981**—President Reagan is shot in the chest in assassination attempt. Sandra Day O'Connor is appointed first woman justice of the Supreme Court.

**1983**—U.S. troops invade island of Grenada.

**1984**—Reagan is reelected president. Democratic candidate Walter Mondale's running mate, Geraldine Ferraro, is the first woman selected for vice-president by a major U.S. political party.

**1985**—Soviet Communist Party secretary Konstantin Chernenko dies; Mikhail Gorbachev succeeds him. U.S. and Soviet officials discuss arms control in Geneva. Reagan and Gorbachev hold summit conference in Geneva. Racial tensions accelerate in South Africa.

**1986**—Space shuttle *Challenger* explodes shortly after takeoff; crew of seven dies. U.S. bombs bases in Libya. Corazon Aquino defeats Ferdinand Marcos in Philippine presidential election.

**1987**—Iraqi missile rips the U.S. frigate *Stark* in the Persian Gulf, killing thirty-seven American sailors. Congress holds hearings to investigate sale of U.S. arms to Iran to finance Nicaraguan *contra* movement.

**1988**—President Reagan and Soviet leader Gorbachev sign INF treaty, eliminating intermediate nuclear forces. Severe drought sweeps the United States. George Bush is elected president.

**1989**—East Germany opens Berlin Wall, allowing citizens free exit. Communists lose control of governments in Poland, Romania, and Czechoslovakia. Chinese troops massacre over 1,000 pro-democracy student demonstrators in Beijing's Tiananmen Square.

**1990**—Iraq annexes Kuwait, provoking the threat of war. East and West Germany are reunited. The Cold War between the United States and the Soviet Union comes to a close. Several Soviet republics make moves toward independence.

**1991**—Backed by a coalition of members of the United Nations, U.S. troops drive Iraqis from Kuwait. Latvia, Lithuania, and Estonia withdraw from the USSR. The Soviet Union dissolves as its republics secede to form a Commonwealth of Independent States.

**1992**—U.N. forces fail to stop fighting in territories of former Yugoslavia. More than fifty people are killed and more than six hundred buildings burned in rioting in Los Angeles. U.S. unemployment reaches eight-year high. Hurricane Andrew devastates southern Florida and parts of Louisiana. International relief supplies and troops are sent to combat famine and violence in Somalia.

**1993**—U.S.-led forces use airplanes and missiles to attack military targets in Iraq. William Jefferson Clinton becomes the forty-second U.S. president.

**1994**—Richard M. Nixon dies in New York City.

# Index

Page numbers in boldface type indicate illustrations.

## About the Author

Jim Hargrove has worked as a writer and editor for more than ten years. After serving as an editorial director for three Chicago area publishers, he began a career as an independent writer, preparing a series of books for children. He has contributed to works by nearly twenty different publishers. His Childrens Press titles include biographies of Mark Twain and Richard Nixon. With his wife and daughter, he lives in a small Illinois town near the Wisconsin border.